MAKING MONEY FROM DOMAIN NAMES
THE DOMAIN FLIPPER'S BIBLE

Amazon Paperback Books,   First Edition
ISBN #978-1-893257-55-9
Copyright 2012   Lions Pride Publishing Co., LLC

TABLE OF CONTENTS

FORWARD

It is an unfortunate fact that books and internet courses are often sold by the pound, not by their content. The idea is to create the perception, the illusion, of value. Don't pre-judge this book by its relatively short length. Generally I find that the longer the material the less likely it is that the buyer will actually read it and apply it.

This book is shorter than many (and thereby *lighter* than many!). I could EASILY have extended it to seventy to a hundred pages and charged $197 or more, and it would contain absolutely zero additional real useful information. None. Zilch. It would simply *look* like it was worth more.

I could use larger type, and I could include "screen shots" of all of the information pages that you can see for yourself by simply going to the many websites presented throughout. I do make the assumption that you know how to find and surf a website!

Personally I find screen shots and "press this button and then press that button" to be insulting. They are included in many books and course manuals as pure fluff designed to add to the weight of the book, the perceived value, but add nothing to the true value. They assume the reader is dumb.

This book attempts to share the wisdom my wife and I have learned over a decade plus of profitable domaining. We presently manage a dynamic portfolio of almost five-hundred domains, and have about three hundred of these monetized. Many others are developed into websites designed to sell a variety of information products and to link to a variety of vendor affiliate programs. Many others are for sale on line and in various auctions.

Domain name investing is slowly replacing all of our other business activities. I fully anticipate that it will support my wife and me throughout our "retirement" years with a minimum of work and a maximum of profit. I can think of no other business that an old poop like me can enjoy and make money at and still savor the good life without a care in the world!

Domain name flipping can be GOD's gift to the work-at-home soccer mom, the student working his or her way through school, or anyone wanting a second income with a minimum of investment of time and money. It is ideal for the retired or semi-retired who may want to supplement their retirement income.

And the best part about it is that it is a lot of fun! If a job is not fun it's not worth doing. Someone once said: "Make your vacation your vocation". Or maybe it was the other way around. Whatever.

I wish the reader nothing but the greatest possible success in this relatively unknown internet business. As easy as it is, you will only get out of it in direct proportion to the effort you put into it. This is true about all internet enterprises.

JUST DO IT!

CHAPTER 1
WHAT'S IN A NAME?

Many of you reading this book already know that a "domain name" is an internet web address, an "http://" or a "www" followed by a " dot [.] something" and a "dot [.]something else". These domain names are also known as "Unique Resource Locators", or "URLs".

These web addresses are the means by which any website is found on a computer. One types the domain name in the appropriate web browser (Internet Explorer, Firefox, or Chrome) search box, hits "Enter", and as if by magic up pops a website! Damn clever I might add.

A domain name can be a single word such as "financial" followed by .com or .whatever, or multiple words such as "financial planning" or "best financial planning" or "the best financial planning"....you get the idea. They can be over fifty characters long!

The evolution of web addresses traces back to various government programs many decades ago (no, Al Gore did <u>not</u> invent the internet). There is actually some disagreement over the exact succession of events and to whom credit should be given. The fact is, it was a tortuous process over many decades involving many individuals before internet web addresses were standardized.

Today, The <u>I</u>nternet <u>C</u>orporation For <u>A</u>ssigned <u>N</u>ames And <u>N</u>umbers (ICANN) has been assigned the responsibility to control most but not all domain name "dot something" extensions. (.ws and a few others are exceptions, and these too may be valuable domain names).

Initially the extensions ".com" for commercial sites, ".gov" for government sites, and .org for academia, came into wide use in the early '90s, followed by ".net" and a few others. Today there are over a hundred ".somethings", such as ".info", ".us", ".biz", ".ws", ".tv", ".mobi", ".ca", ".cn", even ".xxx", and myriad others in additional to the original ones, with new ones added quite often.

In fact, apparently ICANN is going to permit companies and individuals, for a hefty sum, to have their OWN domain extension, such as "GreatProducts.HomeDepot, or "BestDudeEver.Joe Smith". Whatever.

At present there are literally hundreds of millions of domain names already registered worldwide. But that is only a drop in the bucket compared to the many possible domain names that could be conceived and might actually have real value.

There are about 500,000 English language words, and hundreds of millions of possible two, three, four and five or more word combinations.

Multiply that by hundreds of "dot somethings", and then consider the dozens of other common languages, Spanish, French, Italian, German, etc., and one can see that there are almost limitless possible domain names that could be registered and might have value.

This is why the business of flipping domain names is still in its infancy. Every day those in the know are buying domain names and flipping them for multiples of what they cost. But the surface has just been scratched!

Do not make the mistake in believing that you have missed the boat. The boat is still in the dock!

In a few years people will be looking back at today and wishing they had gotten started back in "the good old days", i.e., <u>TODAY</u>! These ARE the good old days. The time for you to get started in this lucrative business is NOW.

The most coveted names are the .coms, followed closely by .nets and .orgs. Recently, .us, .mobi, .info, .biz, and .tv extensions have become saleable commodities. But potentially any extension with the proper wording or phrasing could be a winner.

Remember, each web address is totally unique, one of a kind. Let's say, for example, financial.com is in great demand (in fact it reportedly sold for $100,000). If someone else wants "financial dot something" they will have to settle for one of the extensions other than .com. The more people that want "financial dot something", the deeper into the realm of possible extensions they would need to buy, .net, .org, .info, .biz, etc.

Eventually all the financial dot somethings are taken and the next person will have to pay more to induce one of the owners to sell. Simple supply and demand. Until someone wants your domain name for some reason, it cannot be "flipped". That is not all bad, however, as we will see in a later chapter.

CHAPTER 2
<u>THE FLIPPING BUSINESS</u>

If you are a complete newbie to making money on the internet, the concept of making easy money flipping domain names is as foreign to you as would be an advanced course in website search engine optimization or viral internet marketing.

But if you have had some exposure to internet commerce, perhaps even having purchased an expensive course or two, the concept of making easy money flipping domain names is probably <u>still</u> as foreign to you as to an internet newbie!

You see, few of the well-known internet guru's courses, even the all-time best-selling book on the subject of making money on line, even *mention* the domain flipping concept. The simple fact is that while thousands have pursued conventional internet commerce riches, and many have succeeded, relatively few have focused 100% on domain name flipping.

Just what do we mean by domain name "flipping"? It is a very simple concept. Smaller "domainers" (what the folk who buy and sell domain names and websites are called) like you and me sell to bigger domainers. The beauty of the business is that anyone can participate and make money. It is estimated that there are around 100,000 active domainers.

It is worthy of note that the big players going after vary valuable domains are relatively few, perhaps a hundred or so. This is because very few individuals have the knowledge and experience to evaluate a domain name properly. This fact works to your advantage because you can often sell a domain name or website to the emotionally-driven less-experienced buyers for far more than it may actually be worth.

In conventional real estate, speculators (known as "spec buyers") buy houses that need some sort of enhancement. This might mean mechanical repairs or simple cosmetic painting. Buying spec-houses for below market price for some reason or other, and then selling quickly for profit at a higher price, often *much* higher, is known in the trade as the "flipping" of real estate.

But the flipping of houses most often requires a significant amount of money and risk (with due notice to the "no down payment" gurus), or stellar financial credit, or both. And then there is the expense of the actual rehabilitation, real estate taxes, and insurance. The fact is, it takes a great deal of knowledge and expertise, money and **risk,** to be successful flipping houses.

Domain names on the other hand are *"VIRTUAL Real Estate".* They are under case law real property in much the same sense that a house is real property.

They are not "intellectual property" as is this book.

The big difference between flipping houses and flipping domain names is in the tiny amount of money it takes to get started in the domain flipping business, and the relatively shallow learning curve involved. **The money involved, the work involved, and the risk involved, is minimal.**

So why doesn't everyone do it? A simple absence of wide exposure to the concept explains why. It seems to me that once the secret is out a lot more work-at-home entrepreneurs such as you will get involved, and make their fortunes focusing on domain names.

CHAPTER 3
NAMING DOMAIN NAMES

There are two basic possibilities: original names that you think up off the top of your head, and "secondary market" names that someone in the past thought of that you can purchase from many different sources.

THROUGH ORIGINAL THINKING

It's really very simple. Just pick any word, add words such as "info" and "site" and "best" to make some logical word combination (e.g. "mortgage", "mortgage site", "mortgage info site", "best mortgage info site", etc. Presto, you have a possible domain name!

But before doing any serious buying, go to one of the many websites that list the results of recent on-line auctions and live auctions. From this you can get a really good feel for what dollar amounts domain names can be sold. And you'll get lots of good ideas for your own new domain names as well.

You can find results of recent sales at:

BigSpend at: bigspend.com

Remember, you are only paying only around $10.00 per name for a year of ownership. If you can sit there and think of just five names (which might take an hour if you're really slow) that you can list and eventually sell for perhaps fifty bucks each on eBay, and do this every week, you have just made $10,000 a year for an hour a week of fun! Dedicate more time, buy more domains, and potentially make much more money.

When you search any domain name provider and enter your request, you will see whether or not it is available to purchase.
If you have requested a .com and it has already been registered the site will

show you other major dot extensions that are available.

But more important, most purchase sites will also make related name suggestions that you might never have thought of on your own! This is one of the best idea sources available.

SECONDARY MARKET

There are a great number of websites where you can find domain names for sale. A Google search for "Domain Names For Sale" will turn up dozens. Look at the list below.

You will pay more for a "used" name, often a lot more, but it could be the best investment you will ever make!

Just do it!

CHAPTER 4
<u>BUYING DOMAIN NAMES</u>

When it comes to buying domain names you have thought of yourself, you have a lot of choices. All of the registrars shown below sell original domain names. In fact, there are literally hundreds of registrars approved by ICANN. All of the registrars shown, however, are not created equal. As with most things in life you get what you pay for. There are seldom, if ever, free lunches.

My favorites are godaddy.com and enom.com. Both charge under $15.00/year of ownership for a domain name. All have many useful features and in general offer very hassle-free service. You need to check them all out. It is very important in my opinion to settle on a single registrar that you like, and eventually have all of your domains with that one registrar.

Do *not* be influenced by price, at the high or low end. One of the highest priced I know of, at $35.00 per year for .coms, has given me fits over the years and I have finally transferred all of the domains I manage out of there to a more user-friendly registrar.

Conversely, there are some "$5.00 and less specials" registrars that will drive you equally crazy with unwanted offers before you can even get to the registration process! Some make it very difficult or nearly impossible to transfer domains to another registrar, as you may have to do when you sell a domain.

It took my wife and me almost *two years* of frustration to transfer JesusSonOfGod.com to a friend of mine! It took us five minutes when we sold BuffaloMilk.com at a massive profit. Obviously different registrars!

Some registrars are highly anal retentive.....yearly renewals are how they make their money in addition to the initial registration fee (which is normally the same as the renewal fee). In case I failed to mention it, one can initially register a domain for one, up to ten years, often with a slight discount per year for the longer terms. We have NEVER registered a domain for more than a year. It inspires me to flip my domains quickly!

There are many other valuable services a registrar can offer, *free* multiple e-mail addresses being an important one.

In the paragraphs above we are talking exclusively about new domain name registrations for names you thought of yourself.

The possibility of selling some for many hundreds of dollars, and a few for thousands, and hitting the occasional home run, makes it even more attractive. The sky is literally the limit!

Go to any registrar and see if your "domain word" is available in some form and with some top level domain extension (.com, .net, .org, .mobi, .us, .info, .biz etc.) On most sites, just entering your word or words will immediately pop up a list showing what has already been registered and what is available. Once you get the hang of it you will find it to be a really fun exercise.

Some of the registrars will automatically list many suggestions that relate in some way to what you were seeking in the first place. Remember, they are just trying to sell name registrations, as many and as fast as possible, and will provide you with all the help they can!

Need ideas for domain names as pure speculation? Think of a potential Presidential or Vice Presidential candidate for this election cycle or a future one, and list a number of URLs around that name: Snatorum.com; Newt.com; Romney.com; IloveHillary.com, etc.

In doing so you may get stuck for a time with the unsuccessful candidates (at $10/year), as in RudyForPresident.com or ILoveEdwards.com, but who knows if in 2016 or beyond these could be worth a small fortune!

Olympics in 2020 or 2024? Find the identity of potential city-candidates and register them all in some form. Sure it costs money, but all you have to do is hit ONE winner (LondonOlympics.com for example) and the overall cost becomes of little consequence. But you've got to be fast on your feet......and sometimes a bit lucky. The pros are doing this every day.

There are hundreds of major cities worldwide. It is unlikely you could find any "majorcity".com available, but what about "majorcityshops.com" or "majorcityhotels.com".

There is one very clever way to decide on domain names to register. Follow closely the highest priced domain sales from various auctions. Once you see a domain name sell for thousands or even millions of dollars you <u>at once</u> (or someone out there will definitely beat you to it) begin looking for the identical name, or similar-meaning word combinations, but with lower level domain name extensions.

A good site to follow is bigspend.com. Look for synonyms expressing much the same message. Go for .com first, then .net and .org, then check out .biz, .us, .info, .mobi and continue through the ten most popular extensions. Any one of these, held over time for about $10/year each, could have major value in the future.

The way to do this is to key in words in search boxes at sites such as enom.com or godaddy.com. At no cost they will provide you with a list of available domain names that are similar <u>and</u> available. Whatever you end up registering will not be as attractive or as valuable as the biggie you are trying to closely copy, but in the future they could well be worth far more than your minimal cost.

The domain name "femalemale.com" sold for six figures. We immediately snagged "femalemale.net". We'll see the wisdom of that registration some time in the future!

When you "bank" one or more of these domains you should either "park" them at a monitizer such as fabulous.com (the monitizer I use) or set up a simple Google AdSense site, and then just forget about it. They should bring it over time more money than they are costing you to carry.

CHAPTER 5
<u>SECOND HAND NAMES</u>

Everything we discussed above is based on your *original* ideas. This is by far the least expensive way to acquire domain names.

But you can also buy quality domain names from other owners on-line from an on-line auction sites such as moniker.com or even eBay.com. This is another whole world of domain name buying, the world of the secondary market.

For starters, there is buying on eBay and Craig's list, but we have found these to mostly list overpriced domains offered by individuals who are looking for newbies who don't know domain values and tend to overpay. Worth checking anyway.

You can bid on domains at any of the online auction sites. A word of advice on auctions....if you see something you want ALWAYS try to be the last bidder.

Set a maximum price in your mind and never allow yourself to get into an emotional bidding war. That is a guaranteed way to overpay.

The most important place to buy secondary-market domains is from the drop-list brokers. These brokers publish daily lists of expiring domains. It is reported that upwards of <u>thirty-thousand</u> domains expire daily! That's a lot of potential inventory.

Many of these are domains where the owner may have spent a lot of time and money on a website or traffic and simply forgotten to renew it. We've been guilty of this ourselves I'm embarrassed to say. Some were simply registered and forgotten, dropped through the cracks. We are far more careful today.

Different registrars have different policies on renewal grace periods after expiration. We have lost important domains in the past (We've learned the hard way to be more diligent) because we had them at a registrar that gave us no renewal notice at all and very little if any grace period....remember, all registrars are not created equal.

The key here is to analyze domains in which you have interest in terms of the criteria shown below. Then backorder the same domain at EACH drop broker.

When the domain becomes available if you are the only one ordering it you pay $60.00 and it is yours. I have heard stories of individuals paying $60.00 and flipping it back to the person who let it expire for hundreds of dollars the very next day!

I've also heard stories of individuals who have paid $60.00 for domains with hundreds of links and high Alexi and Google rankings, and flipping these for thousands of dollars within a week.

If you are not the only one that has backordered a particular domain, then a bidding auction begins. I've seen

$61.00 win because the other side doesn't re-bid at all for whatever reason, and I've seen $71.00 take a lot of good domains.

I've also seen bids go into the thousands. A friend of mine paid $20,000 for one of these domains and he tells me it was the best investment he ever made!

Remember one important truism, whether you are buying real estate (e.g., houses) or virtual real estate (domain names) you make your money when you _**buy**_, not when you sell. When you buy at the right price your ultimate profit is locked in and virtually assured.

To summarize, simple buying creatively from registrars and marketing creatively you can make a lot of money with a minimal investment of time and money. But if you want to have a much more time-intensive domain business with greater profit potential, then the secondary market drop brokers are your portal to potential riches.

CHAPTER 6
<u>WHO WANTS MY NAME?</u>

You must understand that the best domain name imaginable is absolutely worthless until someone (and preferably a number of some-ones) decides for whatever reason they simply *must* own it. The significant fact is that today hundreds if not thousands of entrepreneurs have embraced the buying of domain names in the secondary market for a variety of reasons as a serious viable business, and one that can be started on a shoestring and is limited only by the imagination.

It's the next best thing to having a legal money printing press! These days, Virtual Real Estate, domain names, may well be far more attractive than conventional real estate as a short and long term investment. Even though some foreclosed home prices are very tempting, it still takes cash and credit to play the house-flipping game. And houses cost a lot more than ten bucks a year to carry!

Remember, the "U" in URL stands for "Unique". Much as an original oil painting is a one-of-a-kind, so is any domain name a one of a kind. Supply and demand. Marketing 101. Is a unique Rembrandt oil painting inherently worth $50 million? Not to most. But it is to someone, somewhere, for whatever reason. Think "unique".

Is the dot com "SheMale" worth $400,000? It was to someone in January '08. Why? I'm certain the seller could not have cared less! I imagine the buyer had a very good reason.

There are many different reasons why domain names are purchased. The most obvious is pure speculation. You buy it for X$ and flip it to someone for 3X$, who expects to flip it later for 6X$, etc. That person (or you initially) may simply "bank" it, that is, just sit on it until it is flipped in the future. Simple flipping is the easiest way to earn money with domain names. It is an absolute "no brainer" business, which is why my wife and I focused on it for years.

Another reason one might buy a domain name is for "branding" some specific product or idea. We sold "BuffaloMilk.com" to a UK firm that wanted it for a product branding (I cared not at all *what* product, but I sure don't recall ever seeing a herd of buffalo in the UK!).

Yet another possible reason could be the development of a large commercial website somehow related to a particular domain name.

Still another reason to buy a domain name from you is "monetization" (see below for the names of some monitizers) Any name can be "monetized", that is, submitted to any of a number of companies who place relevant advertising on a site they create for the domain owner and share with that owner any revenues generated. These ads can be created for them by Google in a program called "Adsense", or the ads can be created by the monetizing company themselves.

There have even sprung up a number of large conglomerates that exist solely for the purpose of buying up large quantities of domain names for future sale or monitization. Among these are companies reported to be controlled by H. Ross Perot, Richard Rosenblatt (former Chairman of MySpace.com before he sold it to News Corp. for a mere $570,000,000!) and Howard Schultz (Chairman of Starbucks, through his investing firm Maveron). If these kinds of investors are involved you *know* it's a viable market and a place to make real profits.

There is a very wealthy Chinese domain name speculator who has tried quite successfully to corner the market on domain names associated with weddings. He has become very wealthy.

Do you think you could dream up some combination of words that might not already have been conceived and registered that just might be flipable to someone for some multiple of your cost? No reason why you cannot. It's done every day.

Just do it!

CHAPTER 7
WHERE DO I SELL THEM?

A good place to start would be to list your domains on an on-line auction site such as moniker.com. There are other companies such as fabulous.com that not only will monetize your domain name with relevant ads but also list your domains for sale to the general public.

You might also consider trying eBay or Craig's List, but it is my experience that only bargain-hunting bottom-feeders shop for domains there. You would be much better off at one of the auction sites specifically geared to domain investing.

There are even specialty live auctions held worldwide for domains related specifically to a particular topic, such as "casinos and gambling" or "sexual content" or "weddings". And there are general auctions where anything at all might turn up.

These auctions often cost a thousand dollars or more just to attend, and are frequented by hundreds of wealthy domain-investment professionals eager to bid on premium domains! The owners of the domains themselves need not attend the actual auctions to have their domains sold there.

It is worthy of note that a large percentage of domains are sold *privately.* These transactions are seldom reported. This can occur in one of two ways.

It has been my experience that a buyer will contact a domain owner directly, finding the owner's name listed in the WhoIs directory of domain owners. My wife sold VoiceTones.com and TopTenHawaii.com in this fashion. (Side note: Once you own a domain go in to the WhoIs register and after your name as owner add the words "Domain For Sale".)

When you buy a domain name from a registrar you will be offered the opportunity to remain anonymous on WhoIs. This is purportedly to insure your privacy and avoid spam. It also avoids contact from eager buyers! The trade off is well worth it.

A little creative marketing can go a long way. For example, if you owned the name "SanDiegoRealEstate.com" (or any other city, county, or state) dot almost anything you could send an eMail (or, GOD forbid, do a snail-mail broadcast letter mailing) to every licensed real estate agent in San Diego offering the name for sale at some price that you could state or leave open to negotiation. My guess is that one of these agents would snap it up in a heartbeat.

One useful sales technique is to email possible end users of a domain you own. Take a look at paid ads that result from a Google search for a related term.

These ads are usually found at the top or side, apart from the organic search results. Send out simple emails to as many as possible that says: Greetings from (the domain you want to sell). (The domain you want to sell) is available for $(whatever you are asking) at (put a link to sedo.com or wherever it can be bought.) exactly linking to the domain sale page for that domain name. This works well for sale prices under $500.

You might also consider snail-mail to the CEOs of companies directed to their correct name. Addressing your letter to "Company President" is obviously less personalized, but do so if you cannot find the top person's name.

The whole idea is to get your domain name, and the fact that it is for sale, in front of as many domain buyers as possible. This would include these end users, small domain flippers, Wall Street players, and bulk portfolio buyers.

Why wouldn't these companies or real estate agents have not just registered the name themselves? Because most people have not a clue how to go about registering a domain name!

My wife owns the domain MdUV.net, and she plans to some day offer it to every radiologist ("Doctor Ultraviolet") in the country for $50,000! Don't be surprised if she gets it!

Incidentally, the process of selling a domain name can be made vary safe for both buyer and seller through the use of domain name sale escrow company services. Escrow holds the money from the buyer. You do not get the money from escrow until the buyer gets the domain name.

The buyer does not get the domain name until escrow has the funds in their account. Escrow releases the funds to the seller once the buyer owns the domain name. It's a win-win.

I highly recommend that all secondary market purchases from individuals, and all of your sales, go through an escrow service. Most every registrar offers this service. _Never_ buy from or sell to any individual person in the secondary market without this protection. Always protect yourself with a third-party escrow service. The small cost is well worth it.

One _very_ overlooked area is _barter._ There are some fine references on the subject of barter in general …just Google "barter systems". This occurs when you have a domain name someone wants and they have something, anything, that you want.

I recently bartered the domain name PhotographWomen.com for a $6,000 internet training program run by a famous internet guru! The domain name might have been worth more, but I was very happy with the barter exchange because the domain name cost me ten bucks and I wanted that training program!

It is also possible to *swap* domain names. You might own a domain name of which you are not overly fond. Someone out ther in cyber-space might have a domain name you might want badly that they do not especilly care for. Swap time!

There is also the real possibility of *renting out* your domain name. Perhaps a potential buyer might not have the ready cash to buy your domain name, but *could* afford a monthly rental cost of a few hundred dollars. This is exactly the same scenario as with renting real estate.

You could rent the domain name and give the renter the option to buy it at some pre-set price at some specified time in the future. You could also offer as an inducement the possibility of applying all timely rental payments against the ultimate selling price. It is a common real estate strategy that helps close many deals, and it applies equally well to virtual real estate.

The fact is there are many different avenues for making money with your domain names, and very often using a combination of them creatively can yield the greatest reward.

CHAPTER 8
HOW MUCH MONEY CAN I MAKE?

Ah, the magic question! And the one for which attorneys are paid thousands to create disclaimers, like the one at the beginning of this book! Sorry, it just had to be there! Litigation is hell.

<u>The fact is, there is no definitive answer.</u> Somewhere between millions of dollars and nothing at all would be an honestly stated range.

Want to get your wealth juices flowing? Just go to any of the sites shown below (try dnjournal.com for starters) and take a look at prices that are being paid daily for domain names that cost someone $10 or so to register. Do it sitting down!

There is virtually unlimited potential for wealth through various internet commerce pursuits. There are reported to be many thousands of internet millionaires, some of them in their early twenties and some even in their teens. I have no doubt that some brilliant nine-year-old out there somewhere is showing his or her dad how he can retire next year!

I know one young gentleman quite well personally, Anthony Morrison (you can Google him, or click anthonymorrison.com) He is a totally self-made millionaire in his 20s. Amazing young man. True genius. He left med school to save his family from financial ruin caused by the WorldCom debacle. Great true story.

I have met, or have studied under, many other gurus of all ages.....the late, great Cory Rudl who died tragically in his 20's, not long after his wedding ceremony/conference which I attended. There's Dr. Jeffrey Lant; Robert Allen; Mark Joyner; Stone Evans; Sean Mize; Marlon Sanders; Yanik Silver; Armand Morin; Mike Filsame; Jay Abraham; John Reese and many others.

Some if not most of these individuals started with nothing or next to nothing and attribute internet commerce for helping them generate their wealth within the past decade. They are the leaders, the "gurus" of net commerce. They are my idols.

But to the best of my knowledge, with the exception of Anthony Morrison, none of these ever focused their attention on domain names as their **initial** primary business.

I was fortunate to have been introduced to domain name acquisition quite by accident. I attended one of the very early internet commerce presentations on Long Island back in the mid-90s. It was focused on selling products on line. The seminar ended up costing me $2,000…and of course I brought the material home and never opened it!

As an aside, during the presentation the speaker casually mentioned what a cool idea it was to get a .com address containing one's "personal name".com. He said: "You never know, some day it might be worth something." He clearly did not have a clue that the program of selling products that he was pushing was puny in its potential compared to what could have been made buying .com names during those early years.

So I bought the "my name" dot com domain, and a few others that related to various interests of mine. As I recall they cost $35 each to register at that time. At the time very few persons were gobbling up .com domains, and virtually any short English language name .com could be had for a pittance.

A few very lucky souls bought names during that period that sold for up to $4,000,000 each! In fact, Diamonds.com reportedly sold for $7.5 million! That's quite a profit for a $35.00 investment!

Are such opportunities available today? Well, back in January 2008 at auction the dot com "SheMale", acquired rather recently, sold for $400,000!

If you want an extreme example of "the possible", consider the article in the June 2007 issue of *Business 2.0* Magazine.   They ran a cover story titled: "The Man Who Owns The Internet".   That man, quite unknown to most, is Kevin Ham, dubbed "The Master Of Web Domains".

They claimed Mr. Ham has a net worth of $300,000,000.00 and earnes $70 million a year in revenue entirely by being a "Domainer", finding ways to make money through buying and selling and developing domain names. Now that is **serious** money!

How did Mr. Ham accomplish this in less than a decade? He did it starting in the late '90s by systematically buying up a massive portfolio of domain names....300,000 of them! Will you ever buy that many? Unlikely. But you could easily buy a few hundred over time, and earn a very good living from them.

There have been reported dozens of million-dollar-plus sales of individual domain names. One portfolio of domain names is reported to have fetched a mere hundred million dollars ($100,000,000)! That is _serious_ money.

As mentioned elsewhere in this ebook there are many ways to make money by acquiring domain names, and many different ways to acquire them. The simplest and least work-intensive way to earn domain cash is by simply thinking up creative domain names, buying them, and selling them to others as quickly as possible, doing absolutely nothing else but that.

Can you expect to buy a domain name today and flip it for hundreds of thousands of dollars? Highly unlikely, though not entirely impossible. But it _is_ possible to acquire domain names today that can be sold for hundreds, thousands, even tens of thousands of dollars. You just need to know how. A little luck doesn't hurt either!

Do only single-word domain names auction for big bucks? Can seemingly common phrase domain names sell for thousands? For example (and there are many thousands of examples) domains such as: artandframe.com, nextwavewireless.com, marinetechnology.com, marketingmix.com, and fashiongallery.com all sold for $4,000 or more.

Perfectworld.com sold for $30,000. Globalsearch.com sold for $67,000. Even some .net URLs sell well. Take freestuff.net which fetched $28,000 in a Moniker auction as proof.

Highly significant was the report of a recent high-dollar sale of a domain name that had just been registered in a brand new domain name extension. The new extension is ".me", begun in late 2011. The domain name that was registered for ten bucks or so was "meet.me". Damn clever.

Beyond clever is the fact that this brand shiny new domain name was flipped quickly for $450,000.00!!!! That's a fast profit of $459,990.00. So are there possibilities today for instant riches? Apparently so.

Don't expect to read this book and get rich overnight with little or no effort. You actually have to *do* something. It is an absolute fact......and I have personally been guilty of this myself many times......that buying an information product such as this book and not acting on the wisdom contained therein will be absolutely guaranteed to earn you zero dollars. Absolutely guaranteed! No disclaimer necessary.

Every individual has a different level of motivation, a different amount of time to devote to a new pursuit, and a different idea of what "a lot" of money might be. But with average intelligence, a real desire to earn money, and at least a few hours a week to devote initially, domain flipping can be very financially rewarding.

CHAPTER 9
<u>VALUE ENHANCEMENT</u>

As a general rule look to buy domain names that relate to a product in some ways. Ideally, you want to drive traffic to a website from visitors who search generically for the exact domain name. It is called "organic traffic".

Once you own a domain name there are two basic business models: develop a website and sell something, or park the domain it and earn advertising revenue.

For starters, you can just buy "original" domain names and do nothing more with them until you find a buyer. It's very simple, straightforward, and, in fact, pretty much what my wife and I did for years.

I have heard of individuals who daily buy a number of domain names and quickly flip them the same day on eBay and other auction sites for $30.00 to $60.00. Small amounts daily can add up to a lot of profit yearly. A $20/day profit equals $7,200/year per domain name!

In fact, if this was all one did, day trade the same as commodity market day traders or stock market day traders, and all one's domain names sold for an average of $40.00, that's about $50,000 yearly for every five names registered daily.

You do *not* have to hit home runs to make money with domain names. An accumulation of bunt singles can make you rich!

One situation to note here is that the registrar holding your domain names is monitizing them themselves and pocketing 100% of the revenue (it's somewhere in the small print in their Agreements). I'm not sure they all do this, and some may even share revenue with you, but don't count on it. If you just buy and hold, someone else is making some money with ads on a site they created with your domain name.

There are a number of companies that will monitize your domains for you with little or no effort on your part. <u>But all of these monetizing companies are not created equal.</u>

It is a good idea at first to split your domains to be monetized among a number of these monitizers to see which perform best for you. You can always transfer them at a later date. It is a very simple matter to switch your domains between monitizers.

Simply go into your domain name account at your registrar of choice and go to the DNS (Domain Name Server) for your specific domain name and type in the DNS of any monetizer you want to point the name to.

Here again, getting back to the subject of registrars, some make this DNS change very simple, and some make it a royal pain. Choose your registrar wisely.

That all may sound complicated and time-consuming, but once you do it one time it takes less than a minute and a few mouse clicks to point a domain name to a monitizer.

Incidentally, most monitizers have a "sign up for a selling account" process. Some require a certain number of domain names be submitted. Some will only accept higher quality names. Some will accept any domain name at all. They will advise you which sort of domain names are acceptable to them

The ads the monitizers put on the sites for you are relevant to the domain names to take advantage of organic traffic. Some are provided by Google in their "Adsense" program (go to Google.com and search "AdSense" for a full discussion). Other ads are provided by the monitizers themselves.

You won't earn much at first, but over time the domains gather momentum and attract more and more traffic. It's a pure numbers game. You won't get rich letting the monitizers do all the work, but you can earn some extra cash doing absolutely no work.

The above discussion applies to those domain names you thought up yourself and bought from a registrar (which accounts for about 95% of all the domains my wife and I have ever owned).

But for those better expired domain names that you buy in the secondary market at auction, or from drop-companies, you can immediately begin to get revenue in many different ways.

One way is to solicit and sell advertising on your sites. Another is to sell site links. If a domain you buy has a high link rating, and gets, or may get, a lot of traffic, potential advertisers will do back-flips to pay you to run their ads.

The subject of selling links is beyond the scope of this chapter. It is a sophisticated endeavor, and there are many books on the subject. Suffice it to say that if you buy a domain name with a lot of existing backlinks and a lot of existing traffic, you have bought yourself a cash cow!

It would take many months and a lot of knowledge for you to duplicate the page rank and link popularity of many domain names that you can buy from drop companies. Buy one of these and you take advantage of the hard work done by others over time. This is time and effort you do not have to spend.

In summary, there are three basic choices: flip immediately, park for ad revenue, or develop a website. Buying domain names from a registrar or in the secondary market opens up a world of opportunities for creating wealth. You must decide whether you will:

Flip domain names quickly with no enhancements;

Hold the name and develop a website, acquire links, get traffic;

Use your website to sell products or link to affiliate vendors;

Monitize your website with private ads or Google AdSense;

Use your developed website to sell links to others;

Use your domain name at a monitizer for them to run ads;

Rent your domain names;

Accumulate a portfolio of domain names for later use;

Sell entire developed websites;

The easiest business model of all is domain parking at a monitizer. This is simply "set it and forget it" Once you own a domain name, set up and optimize the parking page with keywords, and move on, and on and on.

Simply "rinse and repeat", domain after domain after domain, and let those puppies generate continuous income forever! This is the ultimate lazy marketer's business model, limited only by the number of domains you monetize over time.

Notice I said "almost" the easiest. There are many internet marketers who add no value at all to any domain name they buy. They simply buy creative names for ten bucks and turn around the **same day** and re-sell them to the apparently-limitless universe of eager, largely clueless domain name buyers on eBay. It's a great part time business.

It takes about a minute to buy a domain name, and ten more to list it on eBay. If you buy ten names a day and can sell them for $25 to $40 each, which is very commonly done, well, just do the math yourself. Some devote another ten minutes to listing the domain name with a monitizer and advertise it as an "ad optimized website" which, in fact, it is.

I suggest you watch domain auctions on eBay for a few weeks and decide whether you can make money this way in a few hours a day. You won't get filthy rich with this business model, but you should be able to generate extra cash.

There is a basic blueprint you can follow step-wise that will help you decide a direction in which to proceed:

Park with a monitizer and see what traffic you can get;

If it shows some decent traffic, create a one-page website with three short relevant articles and your own AdSense ads bought through Google directly. The monitizer no longer gets his vig!

If that looks promising, take the next step and create a full-blown website, create products, gather email names, drive traffic, and get rich!

Welcome to the wonderful world of the Domainer!

CHAPTER 10
<u>GREATER VALUE</u>
<u>ENHANCEMENT</u>

Creating a well-optimized website that can be flipped for multiples of what you paid for it will take some time and effort. Enhancing keyword use is one way. There are the five "keyword hotspots" for you to work on:

1. The description and keyword meta tags;
2. A well-written Title Tag.
3. The headline and sub-headline;
4. Within the text;
5. Behind the images.

There are also some additional "enhancements" you should definitely incorporate in the websites you will be upgrading, if these are not already present:

You MUST show **unique** text content on the website. Try to have at least five, preferably ten pages of unique content;

Add a "Privacy Policy" page;

Add an "About Us" page;

Add a "Contact Us" page;

Have links to the above three pages at the bottom of the landing page and every other page;

Add an "Additional Useful Information" page with links to various other short articles.

Include a Site Map page, with links to every other page. This allows Google to easily spider the entire site. Very important.

The landing page content must be targeted and relevant to the keywords on which visitors might be bidding.

Consider including a Resource Page with a link at the bottom of the landing page. This should contain a list of any .edu or .org sites related to the website's niche. This scores big points with Google.

Try to make the site visually more attractive.

Get listed in the DMOZ Directory.

Making all of the above enhancements will go a long way to adding massive value to any tired old pig of a dropped websites. Swans can be worth a fortune!

Incidentally, all else being equal, when you buy a dropped website, look for the age (date of first registration) of the domain name, the older the better. It is one factor in Google's complex rating algorithm.

Your goal is to be able to document real earnings statistics, derived from product sales, ad revenue, affiliate programs, and AdSense ads. Once you achieve this you can price a website at large multiples of recent earnings.

Any potential buyer of your developed website can easily determine all of the analytical statistics about your site, so there is no way to "fake" value. The numbers tell the tale. Savvy buyers and sellers do a SWOT analysis: **S**trengths, **W**eaknesses, **O**pportunities, and **T**hreats.

You have a wonderful opportunity to create and flip websites on which you are "promoting" an ebook or a .pdf downloadable report of some sort. You sell the website **together with** exclusive worldwide rights to the book itself. From the results I am seeing the very creation of the site, with no effort aimed at traffic or sales for the book or report, is enough to make a huge profit.

Study the auction site Flippa, at flippa.com. It is a website marketplace. From what I see $400 to $900 is a common purchase price for such a website. Your cost? The $10 cost of a domain name, and the time it takes you to find a copyright-free government publication and put it on a simple website. Add to this the time to create a killer book cover, the time for keyword research for your website, and the time it takes to put up the simple website.

No clue how to create an article, or a book cover, or a simple website? Go to fiverr.com and for five dollars each have someone else do it for you!

Five-hundred bucks or so seems like a lot of money to earn in return for a $10 to $25 investment and a couple of hours of work, and it is!   And you can do this over and over and over……………

A key to this is registering a domain name that is identical to some popular

Google search term, and naming the ebook accordingly. If you can generate some traffic or show some sales statistics, the sky can be the limit on your sales price!

Note that ICANN will not allow a domain name transfer from your registrar to anywhere for sixty days after registration. You can always point your domain name to the servers where you are having your site hosted during this time period.. It becomes a problem if you sell a domain name within those sixty days if the buyer wants it transferred to his hosting company.

The entire world of domains is changing with the recent advent of "dot anything and everything". This is expected to become effective in 2013. Big brands will now have websites at .macys or .lowes. Only time will tell what effect this will have on the traditional top level domain (TLD) popularity.

I still believe that .com will always be the key "domain brand", just as Xerox and Kleenex and Chlorox will always mean "a copy", "a tissue", and "a bleach".

It is reported that there are around a quarter billion (250,000,000) domain names registered across all of the TLDs. Roughly half of these are .com and .net combined, with .com by far the most important.

At the end of the day the only valuation that matters at all is the one done by your prospective buyers who have both the desire and the liquid funds to buy your site. People are willing to pay high prices to avoid having to develop sites themselves, or perform search engine optimization, or identify profitable niches, or drive traffic to a website.

But value, as with beauty, is entirely in the eyes of the beholder. There simply is no exact valuation for any domain name or website. The most accurate valuation you can get online seems to come from ebizvaluations.com which employs not some vague math algorithm but uses prices for which hundreds of similar sites have historically sold.

Flipping websites is a very profitable business model. Most seasoned internet marketers understand, however, that the flipping business model is NOT the most profitable for most of us. Developing websites and selling our own unique products and affiliate products to a huge universe of double-opt-in email subscribers trumps flipping. It's just a lot harder.

The most consistently successful domainers employ the develop, hold and market business model. Simply flipping raw unenhanced websites can leave too much potential earnings on the table.

In any event, I strongly recommend that you go to each of the above sites and study every aspect of them before you even think about flipping domain names or developed websites. Note in particular what final prices different sites sell for. Imagine yourself participating in the action.

There are many internet entrepreneurs who focus on this one business model alone and make a fortune doing it. There is no reason why you cannot become one of them. It takes time and patience but it can be one the most profitable of the many multiple streams of internet income.

Just do it!

CHAPTER 11
WHAT'S MY DOMAIN NAME WORTH?

For starters, let's review the factors that create value in a domain name. All of these factors are considered in the algorithms used by the appraisal services (see below) to determine value estimates.

First of all, the extension, .com, .net or .whatever, is a critical matter.

Because it is the oldest commercial dot something, and the most highly recognized, the entire domain and internet commerce industry has been dubbed "The Dot Com Revolution". You've heard of the "Dot Com Bubble" where stocks in highly inflated internet startups (which had nothing whatever to do with a .com domain name) dropped sharply in value almost overnight.

The revived current internet realm is often referred to generically as "dot com two" (.com2). "DotCom" has become the generic vernacular for the internet industry, "the dot com industry" as a whole.

And because of this name recognition, and the public perception that a company with a .com website has probably been around a longer time (which may or may not be the case, but perception is everything), the .com extensions for a given word or phrase command a premium price.

Next most recognized is .net, followed by .org, and the more recent .mobi, .info, .us, .biz and .tv. One only has to look at auction results to get a sense of the relative number of .com sales compared to any other extension.

This is not to say that the others cannot have value in the tens of thousands of dollars. They can and often do. It is just that if we compare apples to apples .com extensions are worth much more than the other extensions.

Equally important is the number of letters in the word before the dot something. One- and two-letter and most three-letter words (as well as all letters of the alphabet) were registered in most TLDs (the Top Level Domains, which includes all seventy or so ICANN dot somethings) many years ago. These are generally prohibitively expensive when they do appear for resale.

Occasionally one can snag a dropped four or five letter word domain name, but that is rare. In fact, finding any single-word .com that could relate to some product that has not already been registered is virtually impossible today. If you want to waste an hour grab a dictionary and try to buy any three-letter or four-letter dot com domain name based on a common English language word. You will quite quickly see what I mean.

You can even make up three and four letter acronyms, nonsense words, and you will still find them all gone bye bye. Single-word domains, the shorter the better, and .com, .net, .org, .mobi, .info, .us, .biz and .tv are worth the most, but are very hard to come by.

Then we have two-word domain names, again, the shorter the better.   And the combination should make sense. "BestFood" would be worth vastly more than "FoodSand" if you get my drift. Here again, a good three-word domain name such as "BestOrganicFood" would be more valuable than a two-word nonsense phrase.

When we get beyond three words the domain name may be very useful to someone trying to brand something but is not as easy to sell. My wife a while ago acquired a very fine site for offering major credit cards: PremiumCardOffersOnLine.info. That domain name itself would have little value in the secondary market (which is not to say the entire website might not have value, but that is a different matter.)

It must be noted here that hyphenated words such as "Best-Organic-Foods" may be worth as much as the same domain name words without the hyphen. The thinking among those who feel this is true is that hyphenated domain names are easier to read. Those who do not believe in hyphenated names feel that buyers would tend to omit the hyphens and end up at a different website.

Abbreviations such as "4" for "four", "biz" for "business", etc. definitely diminish value.

Certain numbers and number combinations of particular note, "666", "777", "711", "911", or any single or two digit number dot com, would be extremely valuable, but these were registered years ago and have very high worth today.

Many internet marketers have a sort of "gray hat" way of earning internet income. They register common misspellings of popular website domain names. The idea is to profit (usually through AdSense ads on their sites) from traffic they get because the misspelled search term is entered into a search engine's search box.

Just for kicks try misspelling the domain name of some popular site. Chances are quite good that you will land on an AdSense site. These sites do get traffic. For example enter "weeding" instead of "wedding". "forevlosure" instead of "foreclosure" (note v is next to c on your QWERTY keyboard). My wife owns "noageing.com". I'm not sure we knew that the correct spelling is "aging" when we registered it! I recently (intentionally) registered: "JamaicanIndependance.com". Sure looks right to me. It ain't!

The free download "Domain Name Analyzer" at domainpunch.com has a feature called "Traffic Finder" which can be used to research misspelled domain names.

I know another internet marketer who makes a very good living selling domain names directly on Craig'sList. He takes advantage of their geographic-targeted feature. He chooses a city, registers names such as (city)hotels.com, or best(city)realestate.com.

Then he emails every hotel or real estate company in that city and asks them whether they would like to purchase this very special unique and valuable domain name! He often gets a thousand dollars or more for his $10 investment and an hour's worth of emails. Awesome!

As a generality, the "memorableness" (I think I just made that word up!) of a word or phrase is counted highly in the valuation algorithm. (Memorability?)

Keep in mind, however, that simple domain buying and flipping has worked for my wife and me for years. Just good words and phrases and aggressive marketing can net thousands of dollars for a minimal investment.

I have found a useful indicator of comparative value to be a limited-daily-use free site located at valuation.com. They come up with an "appraisal" that is of very little relevance to what one might be able to get for a particular domain name, but can be of some use in comparing similar domain names. Their algorithm for evaluation is based on "organic traffic" (a searcher typing in the exact domain name).

The fact is, there is **absolutely no agreement** on the value of a particular domain name amongst the various appraisal companies. For example, my wife owns EgyptianPapyrus.com. I have a written appraisal of $22,000! I also have five other written appraisals of this name between $700 and $2,300.

All appraisals were obtained on the same day but from different appraisal services. The point is that a domain is worth what someone is willing to pay for it, and domain appraisals are, for the most part, <u>totally worthless.</u> This is why I will never allow a buyer to insist on an appraisal, especially if they expect me to pay for it.

I offer the buyer the above example and they usually get the message. If they still insist, I suggest you find a different buyer.

Some last thoughts on the value of domain names. My wife has used the value of her domain names, both estimated values and those values based on written domain name appraisals as valued assets stated on balance sheets in successful loan applications.

Domain names are legally real property, and showing a few million dollars of potential domain name sales value for an entire portfolio , especially with written appraisal documentation, can go a very long way towards making an iffy personal balance sheet look fabulous!

A valuation that is an accepted generality in the industry is that a highly- developed multi-product website is worth twenty-four times (two years of monthly earnings) its median monthly earnings. Such a website that shows a $6,000/month median earnings over a long period of time would be valued at $144,000. This can make a balance sheet's assets really stand out!

A website selling only a few virtual products might be valued at just two times its median monthly sales. A twenty-four month time frame for sales statistics is generally desired by buyers, and required by lenders.

But it is also possible that a website might be worth far more than its earnings indicate, based on its double-opt-in visitor base which may not have been fully exploited. Email lists are pure gold. You can check out ebizvaluations.com for a FREE estimate of the value of a website based on an algorithm taking into account multiple factors.

You don't have to actually BUY a domain name to build yourself a profitable website. LeaseThis.com is the Hertz-Rent-A-Car of domain names! They provide you with the option to lease or rent a domain name for a flat monthly fee for a predetermined length of time, often with the option to buy. In so doing website owners can test the name for traffic and branding purposes without risking a large investment. Slick!

Believe it or not there is even a domain name pawn shop called DigiPawn. Go to digipawn.com and check it out. They loan money on their valuation of your domain names and websites!

Buy, sell, rent, lease, barter, swap, quick flip or develop are all ways to make money with domain names.

Just do it!

CHAPTER 12
<u>WHAT A HIGH-STAKES BUYER WANTS</u>

A domain's value is most frequently based on the actual revenue it produces, averaged over time. That is something that is real and quite predictable. Essentially everything else, aside from verifiable traffic, is nothing more than hot air.

Revenue notwithstanding, the number of monthly visitors does factor significantly into the value of a site. A site receiving fewer than 2,000 visitors/month might be worth a thousand dollars, while one with 30,000 visitors a month might be worth $3,000. Hit 50,000 a month or more and six figures is possible.

By creating traffic you have saved the buyer a great deal of trouble and time, and time to a wealthy website buyer is money. Many short but traffic-developed websites with high traffic have sold for six-figures

Blog sites are less attractive to buyers because they require a constant flow of content to keep traffic and revenues growing. The other side of the coin is that blogs may be easier for you to generate higher traffic figures than constant-contact sites. Static sites are reported to sell for 30% more than blog sites all else being equal.

The most profitable domains for resale are those that are **NOT** tightly niche-focused, but those with the broadest search parameters. Buyers want as many people as possible typing those terms into their browser bar.

A buyer willing to pay large sums for a domain takes many factors into consideration. Though it is highly unlikely that all twenty of the following items would be present in any single website transaction, the more that are present the more a buyer is likely to pay you for the website:

A .com domain name, preferably one where the same name .net and .org and other extensions are part of the sale. This limits future competition.

An aged domain that has never been allowed to expire.

An aged site with a long earnings history.

A large number of backlinks from a wide range of domains.

Links from .edu and .gov domains.

High Google PageRank.

Low Alexa ranking, preferably under 100,000.

A very large database of double-opt-in subscribers.

A valuable demographic, e.g., adult professionals as opposed to pre-teenagers.

Opportunity for the buyer to further monetize the site;

High Cost to recreate the site;

High quality content, the more the better;

Low expenses relative to gross profit;

Multiple sources of earnings;

A source of earnings that requires little regular work.

A loyal visitor base that makes repeat purchases.

Level of post-sale buyer involvement by the seller.

A built-up social community, forum, or blog, with wide participation.

A "beautiful" site can help, even though a buyer can easily have any site re-designed as seen fit.

As you can see from the above list of enhancement factors, a six or seven figure website will take some considerable time to develop. But always keep these factors in mind as a **goal** in connection with any of your developing websites.

In negotiating a large sale there are other considerations that can help to seal the deal:

Will you as the seller accept partial payment with the balance contingent upon the buyer's achievement of some pre-determined goal?

Will you accept installment payments?

Will you offer to be a consultant for some period of time?

Will you sign a "no-compete clause" in the sale agreement?

If the site sells some unique products or book copyrights which you own, will you consider selling the exclusive rights to that product or copyright along with the website?

Are you interested in selling/retaining a part-ownership?
From your standpoint as seller a pure "cash & walk away" deal is preferable. This is not always possible. You may need to offer compromises, or walk away from the deal entirely and seek the all- cash/no contingency buyer you hope is out there somewhere.

A bird in the hand, however, is often worth two (or more!) in the bush. Remember the old Wall Street adage: "Pigs get slaughtered".

Just as with a house for sale, a domain name or a website is **ONLY WORTH WHAT <u>SOMEONE</u> OUT THERE IS WILLING TO PAY FOR IT.** Not a penny more. Not what **YOU** think it's worth. This is a truism that one must accept, and do everything possible to find the right "someone".

Also keep in mind that your sales pitch to the prospective buyers must be highly professional with details about the business and full disclosure of all available statistics. And stating a good believable reason why you are selling the website never hurts.

As pointed out in the preceding chapter, "Name Drops" such as exody.com, pool.com, snapnames.com and justdropped.com are a source of endless opportunities to find potentially profitable domain names both unused and semi-developed or even fully-developed. Great places to flip your websites are eBay (for low end sales to inexperienced buyers), sitepoint.com, and digitalpoint.com.

CHAPTER 13
<u>KEY WEBSITES FOR</u>
<u>DOMAINERS</u>

<u>General Information:</u>

DNJournal.com

Icann.org

GenericDomainNames.
com

UKreg.com

IwebTools.com (to
check for a Google site-
ban)

DomainPunch.com
("Domain Name
Analyzer")

DomainTools.com
($50/month intelligence)

Bizbuysell.com

Domain Research:

Alexa.com   (Link Popularity)

Google.com (Page Rank and Link Popularity)

Yahoo.com   (Link Popularity)

MSN.com   (Link Popularity)

AllTheWeb.com   (Link Popularity)

AltaVista.com   (Link Popularity)

DomainProfiteer.com (For DMOZ listing)

WayBackMachine.com

(History of website content)

Google.com   (Google Cache for website histories)

Domaining.com (See historic sale prices)

DomainPunch.com (Many domain tools)

Domainstate.com (Valuable suite of FREE tools)

Where To Buy Domain Names (registrars/hosts):

GoDaddy.com (I find the least expensive.)

ENom.com (BulkRegister.com)

NameCheap.com

Moniker.com

Dynadot.com

1and1.com

NameSecure.com

NetworkSolutions.com

PurchaseYour.com

Sedo.com "World's Largest Domain Marketplace"

PremiumDomains.com

Name Drops: Exody.com

Pool.com

Snapnames.com (recently merged with   Moniker.com)

JustDropped.com (my favorite)

DomainersEdge.com

ExpiredDomains.com

NameSpy.com

Aftermarket.com

Live Auctions: Moniker.com

NamePros.com

Private Sales: CraigsList.org

EBay.com

URL Appraisers: Afternic.com

Sedo.com

Estibot.com

GoDaddy.com

Valuation.com

BulkRegister.com

NamePros.com

DnScoop.com

LeapFish.com

On-line Auctions:

Sedo.com
(GreatDomains.com)

Afternic.com
(BuyDomains.com)

Moniker.com
(DomainSponsor.com)

TDnam.com
(GoDaddy.com)

PremiumDomains.com
(Mocus.com)

SnapNames.com

Pool.com

ENom.com
(BulkRegister.com)

Domaining.com

PremiumDomains.com

Sell Websites: WebsiteBroker.com

BuySellWebsites.com

Flippa.com (Excellent "Just Sold" info)

Monitizers: Domainapps.com, (formerly whypark.com)

Fabulous.com

NameDrive.com

DomainSponsor.com (Moniker)\

Sedo.com (Best site to sell your domains.)

Parked.com
Afternic.com (It is reported that their process for selling and transferring your names is cumbersome.)

Moniker.com

Escrow Services:

BulkRegister.com

Moniker.com

eBay.com

Escrow.com

Forums: DNforum.com (good for small sales)

NamePros.com (Also buy and sell domains)

DomainState.com

WebmasterWorld.com

WebHostingTalk.com

DomainSalesMachine.com

AcornDomains.co.uk

Pawn Services: DigiPawn.com

Valuation: EbizValuations.com

WebsiteWorth.info

Cubestat.com

EstimURL.com

Bizmp.com

Blogs:

DomainSalesMachine.com

DomainBits.com

DomainSherpa.com

Domainnews360.com

TheDomains.com

Sevenmile.com

<u>Domain News:</u> Dnjournal.com

Domaining.com

DomainNews.com

DomainNameNews.com

Dotsauce.com

DomainNameWire.com

<u>EVENTS:</u> Dncalendar.com

DomainSherpa.com/domain-name-events/

The above sites are listed in no particular order, and are far from complete. They are sites with which the author has had some experience. You can Google search any category for many other sites to explore. You should definitely spend a few days studying all of these sites to get a thorough feel for the business of buying and selling domain names.

NOTE: Domain addresses are NOT letter-case-sensitive. Any combination of lower-case and capitals works exactly the same. The exception is when certain suffixes are seen after a URL that has been shortened or cloaked. At the tail end you will see something like xxxxxxxxxxxxxx.com "/T7HjuY". This special end- extension IS case sensitive.

CHAPTER 14
THE FLIPPING BUSINESS REVISITED

This chapter reviews some of the above material.

You can make a lot of money buying and selling domain names without ever taking the step of creating or enhancing websites. But there is no question that with patience and a knowledge of website creation and optimization you can make far greater profits selling entire operating, proven, money-making websites.

We talked about domain name auctions in the preceding chapter. Many of the domain names that are sold have never been developed into viable websites. But the ones that drew huge prices were almost always proven winners, with many backlinks and high PageRanks and demonstrated profits.

By developing a website and driving traffic to it, the domain name does not only have the potential or perceived value of a "raw" URL, but it has proven conclusively to have <u>real market value.</u>

This value can be established by showing Alexa rankings and Google analytics. You show me a website with an Alexa ranking of 50,000 or lower with tons of traffic and hundreds of relevant backlinks (other websites with links that point to it) and a Google PageRank of 5 or better and I'll show you a website that could easily fetch six figures at auction.

The individuals I know who make large sums of money flipping websites often do so by purchasing dropped domain names that <u>already</u> have some proven history. It can save a year or more of development of a domain name. There are countless domain names that come up for sale every week that have backlinks and a solid history of attracting traffic.

There are many dropped domain names associated with defunct web sites for sale every day. If you can locate a few of these every week that have some documented history, and find yourself to be the only bidder (rare) or one of very few bidders, and not pay a sum beyond your budget for such a domain name, you may have found the royal road to internet riches.

Frequently sites such as these can be purchased for $60. If there is a single other bidder for the domain they may drop out somewhere before the $100 level. Many eBay domain flippers stick to a single $60 bid as their business model.

Those who have a great deal of experience flipping websites are often willing to pay many thousands of dollars for a dropped domain name with a solid history. They know with some certainty from experience what profit they can expect after enhancement.

Searching the various auction sites can provide you with many historic full-website sales prices to give you some sense of the possible. Entire websites are often sold in eBay auctions. This is the "buy for $60, do minimal enhancement, and flip for a few hundred dollars above cost " business model crowd. Many individuals make a very good living in this manner with a minimum of effort.

Fast "cleaning up", i.e., enhancing a defunct site for eBay listing is generally just a matter of optimizing keywords and applying sound principals to make the site visually attractive.

It is analogous to adding value to a beat-up house by making minor repairs such as applying a fresh coat of paint and flipping it ASAP. The added value is far greater than the cost of the enhancements.

Be CERTAIN to check whether a website you are planning to buy has not been **banned** by Google. I was burned once this way myself. I have learned to check this out on iwebtools.com. Always check out every advertised statistic for yourself. Many sellers puff up the numbers, or fabricate them out of thin air!

When selling a low-cost site on eBay advertise it as a "Premium Website". Offer "No Transfer Fees", "Best Deal", "Free Push On (name of a registrar)". "Pushing" is the act of transferring ownership of a domain name/website held at a particular registrar where BOTH buyer and seller are registered with that registrar. It greatly facilitates the transaction.

Be certain to mention in your eBay ad all of the ways you can possibly imagine that the buyer could make money with it in the future. "Perfect for (blah, blah, blah)". Get the picture?

There are many ways to quickly add to a website's value. One quick way is to have the website dedicated to Google

Adsense advertising. You will add some relevant keyword-rich articles, and develop as many "backlinks" from other websites as possible. Frequent blog posts to the site are also important. Then just leave the rest to Google. This is the best eBay model.

The big bucks will not be achieved on eBay where the buyers are generally bargain hunters with a few hundred dollars to spend. To enhance websites with an eye on the big-time auction sites there are many factors to consider in turning a pig into a swan.

Just do it!

CHAPTER 15
DOMAIN RESEARCH TOOLS

When buying domains in the secondary market, there are many factors to consider. The following research tools, listed above, are invaluable in helping you decide which domain names to buy in the secondary market.

ALEXA RANKING: Alexa collects data on website traffic. To check the Alexa ranking of a domain name go to Alexa.com/siteinfo. Any ranking under 4,000,000 is actually considered quite good (remember, there are tens of millions of domain names registered). Any ranking around 1,000,000 is very, very good; under 500,000 is great. Anything under 100,000 is a super valuable gem!

In general, the lower the Alexa ranking the more it will be worth (and the more it will cost to buy). Of course, for any original domains you have bought with ideas from your own mind there will be no Alexa ranking at all, until the site is monitized or developed, and some time passes.

This does not mean "original" unranked domains have no value. Quite the opposite is true. In fact almost all of the domains we have sold over the years have been original-thought registrations, some for many thousands of dollars. And they had **no** Alexa or Google ratings.

In these cases the buyer wanted the "unused" domain name to brand some product or idea and did not care about existing traffic. Of course they would have preferred that the domain had lots of historic traffic, but if it did they would have had to pay lots more dollars to acquire it.

GOOGLE PAGE RANK: Go to Google.com. Type in: cache: (domain name).This is a highly industry-respected indicator of a domain name's importance compared to other domain names on the web. It is a single-integer 1 to 10 scale (1, 2, 3….), but it is not linear. That is to say a "2" is not twice as important as a "1". It is a logarithmic scale, like the Richter earthquake scale.

A "2" Google page rank is 10 to <u>100</u> times better than a "1". (For comparison The Richte scale is only progressive in tenths, 1.1, 1.2, etc, with each tenth 10 times greater than the previous.)

A Google page rank of 3 is good, 4 is very good, and 5 is excellent. Anything 6 and above is a rare gem! But to even attain a Google page rank of "1" is a fair achievement.

<u>LINK POPULARITY:</u> This statistic will tell you how many links from other websites the domain has acquired, the more the better. Go to: advertising.yahoo.com/article/yahoo-web-analytics.com.

A site with under a hundred links is not extraordinary. A link total of 500 is very good, over 1,000 excellent. Some sites have tens of thousands of links!

SITE CONTENT: If you are buying a secondary market domain name for the purpose of a specific idea or product promotion, the relevance of the past and present content on that domain is important. Two ways to find this are: Google: google.com (type "cache"+domain name) WayBackMachine: waybackmachine.com has cached historic   content of millions of websites.

SPECIAL LISTING: dmoz.com. The "DMOZ Open Directory Project" is a manually-processed directory of domains. To be included DMOZ participants must show a domain to have valid relevant content. Being DMOZ listed makes a website and its associated domain name more valuable.

It is important to search all of these sites to familiarize yourself with the available tools. Spend lots of time "drilling down" in the sites to learn as much as you possibly can. Knowlewdgew is power!

Just do it!

CHAPTER 16
<u>CONCLUSIONS</u>

This report is intended to provide a working overview of the domain name industry as my wife and I have participated in it for a decade. Spend some time learning from it, and you may be surprised at how much fun it can be to make money rather easily sitting at your computer. Along the way you might just get rich!

The myriad nuances and branches of the domain name business could fill many volumes such as this, and we surely do not "know it all". In fact, because of our focus on "flipping" to the exclusion of all else the domain name business has to offer, we have probably "left on the table" tens if not hundreds of thousands of dollars in the past. No longer. We try to learn from our past stupidity!

People reminisce about "the good old days" when they could have bought a stock or a piece of land dirt cheap that would have been worth a fortune today. Well guess what……in virtual real estate these *are* (almost) the good old days. Every year you own and hold a domain name is another year it can grow in value.

Domain names get increasingly scarce as more and more are registered every day. Supply and demand. Marketing 101.

Profitable investing in Domain Names is one of the internet's most closely guarded secrets. It is impossible not to get excited when one realizes that the likes of Perot and Schultz and Rosenblatt are reported to have gotten into the act!

But the fact is that the playing field is so huge, and the opportunities so varied, that literally anyone of average intelligence and a small budget can get started this very day on what could be a fun and extremely profitable lifelong adventure!

Don't be one of those people who look at this domainer opportunity and make the mistake that it is too late in the game to get started. The time is NOW to take advantage of one of the internet's best kept big-money-making secrets.

From the looks of things today this Domain Flipping business is still in its infancy, and today's opportunities seem limitless. You have little to lose and potentially much to gain by getting involved at once.

The domain name you fail to register today will probably end up in someone else's portfolio tomorrow, and the profits from flipping that domain will end up in in someone else's bank account a year from now. It might just as well be in your account!

JUST DO IT!

ABOUT THE AUTHOR

Fifteen years ago Burt saw the unlimited potential in internet commerce and especially domain name flipping. It was the ultimate work-from-home entrepreneurial challenge. He decided to make it his primary source of income, as it is to this day.

He's in now in his 75th year of life, which he believes qualifies him as an official "old fart"! Directly involved in internet commerce since 1997, this also qualifies him as "very old" in terms of the age of internet commerce. We cannot think of anyone else even near his age who has the combined internet and lifetime successful business experiences Burt has had. Internet knowledge, learned from the greats and refined through experience, makes him an invaluable domaining resource.

Most of the "old time" internet geniuses, today's well-known internet super-gurus, are now only in their forties and fifties.

Burt has kids that old! These gurus are folks who mostly had successful business careers but tired of the nine-to-five and saw the internet and domaining as a profitable escape. Many became fabulously wealthy.

A brand new age of internet entrepreneurs literally grew up in the post dot-com-bust era. Most of these are <u>still</u> only in their late teens and twenties! Most started with nothing and many today are multi-millionaires. A case in point is the amazing young internet guru Anthony Morrison: (anthonymorrison.com).

Burt says of Mr. Morrison: "I still learn a great deal from him. I was honored a few years ago to have been asked by him to do a TV domain-flipping thirty-minute -infomercial at CBS studios in Orlando. It's quite an ego trip to see oneself on late-night cable TV talking about one's domaining successes!"

Burt is a graduate engineer of the Polytechnic Institute of Brooklyn (now NYU-Poly). He earned an MBA in Marketing from Baruch College - CCNY. Both degrees were earned in night school while he worked daytime jobs to pay for all of his tuition. No loans, no scholarships, just nine years of long hours and hard work.

As a teenager, he became one of the first one-thousand members of American MENSA, the high IQ society, in which he is active to this day. A private pilot, Burt served in a Civil Air Patrol rescue unit. He is a Vietnam era Army veteran and a proud active member of American Legion Post 66 in Green Valley, Arizona.

Over the years he did the "corporate thing", rising to high-level executive positions in three Fortune 500 Divisions. His expertise was marketing- oriented. A published author since 1970, he is responsible for authoring eleven books and countless articles. He has even been published in *Leaders* magazine, which is distributed only to heads of state and CEOs!

Today he and his wife of 29+ years live in absolute paradise on a twenty-acre ranch bordering millions of acres of State lands in the High Sonoran Desert in sunny southern Arizona, along with their two great pups. They have a beautiful 5,570 square foot stone home, have travelled the world, and have every creature comfort they could ever want. Burt attributes it all to internet commerce and especially to **domain name flipping.**

He has no pressing need to continue his daily internet work. Someone once said: "Make your vocation your vacation". Burt really does enjoy doing the tasks that are needed to earn domaining money on the internet, and to teach others to be successful, and plans to do it 'till the end of his days.

Burt says: "If I can help others, especially the unemployed and under-employed to improve their lives through domaining, great! If I can interest seniors such as myself in supplementing their retirement incomes that would be really wonderful. Can I make life financially easier for stay-at-home moms and dads? I hope so. If I can show college students how they can eliminate their loan debt and retire by age thirty I'd feel quite good about that as well."

"Personally, regardless of how much money I earn through domaining it will never be enough. My dreams of creating an enduring charitable foundation to fund a worthy cause will require as much as I can ever earn. I need quite a few domaining millions to make a real dent in that project. It's a five-year plan. And it will happen."

We sincerely hope it does, and have no doubt at all that it will

ADDENDUM

No book about domain names would be complete without a mention of the many "dot somethings" that exist today. Everyone is familiar with ".com", which has become the generic name for the entire internet industry. Most know that ".net" and ".org" exist, but few are aware that there are at least TWENTY generic "Top Level Domains" (TLDs). Beyond that there are dozens of "Country Code" Domains.

The .com and .net TLDs are operated by VeriSign Global Registry Services. They are the best recognized, and from a "flipping" standpoint generally the most valuable.

The .org TLD is operated by the Public Internet Registry. It was intended to serve the non-commercial community, but it is available for anyone to register.

The .edu TLD is registered through Educause. It is reserved for post-secondary institutions accredited by any agency listed on the U. S, Department of Education's list of "Nationally Recognized Accrediting Agencies".

The .gov top level domain, administered by the General Services Administration, is exclusively for the Unite States Government.

The .name TLD is operated by the Global Name Registry and is reserved for individuals.

The .mobi top level domain, sponsored by "mTLD Top Level Domain Ltd.". It was intended to be aimed at providers of mobile device services. Until (and if ever) mobile device makers make .mobi the default extension for all mobile devices this TLD has little special application or value.

The .biz TLD, run by NeuLevel, Inc., was intended for businesses, but can be registered by anyone.

The .info TLD is a "catch all" for domain names unavailable in the better-known TLDs. It is operated by Afilias Ltd.

The .ws TLD is run by Global Domains International. Rapidly growing in popularity and available to anyone, it has been noted as meaning "World Site" or "Web Site".

The .jobs TLD sponsored by Employ Media LLC is exclusively for human rewsource managers.

The .mil TLD is operated by the U. S. Department of Defense and is exclusively for the United States Military branches.

The rarely encountered .int TLD is reserved for organizations established by international treaties between soverign governments. It is administered by the IANA .int Domain Registry.

The .aero TLD is sponsored by SITA (Societe Internationale de Telecommunications Aeronautiques). It is reserved for members of the air-transport industry.

The .coop TLD is run by the Dot Corporation, and is reserved for cooperative associations.

The .museum TLD , sponsored by the Museum Domain Management Association is reserved, not surprisingly, for museums!

The .travel TLDS, reserved for travel-industry entities, is sponsored by Tralliance Corporation.

The .pro TLD is restricted to credentialed individuals. It is operated by RegistryPro.

The obscure .cat TLD, run by Fundacio puntCat, is reserved for the Catalan linguistic and cultural community.

As recently as 2011 the .xxx TLD was created for the porn industry! With an estimated $3,000/SECOND spent on pornography, it was expected to be a hit! It is administered by The ICM Registry.

Aside from the above list of "generic" TLDs, virtually every country on the planet has their own domain name. Most websites having these extensions are in the language of the individual country. There are exceptions, brought about mostly by clever marketing by purveyors of domain names.

The .co domain extension has been touted as an "easier to remember .com", or "company", and heavily promoted. It is the TLD of the Republic of Columbia.

Recently someone at "doMEn Company" in Montenegro got the brilliant idea to replace their .yu extension (Yugoslavia) with .me. This became an instant hit in America with the registration of anything clever such as:

love.me; u4.me so.me and such. We are a "me" society, and this domain extension apparently appeals to the narcissist in us all!

Another popular and fortuitous domain extension is .tv. It has nothing whatsoever to do with television, being the country domain for Tuvalu, administered by Tuvalu-To-Run-TV-Registry.

Not to be outdone, the .ec domain was touted as ".E Commerce". It is actually the country domain for Ecuador, administered by NIC-EC!

So the recent: .co, .me, .tv, and .ec are not: "company", "myself", "television" and "e-commerce", but are: Columbia, Montenegro, Tuvalu and Ecuador! I don't recall seeing that disclosure in the endless ads for these domains.

From the viewpoint of a profitable domain name business, there is no question that .com is now and probably will be forever the best-recognized and most valuable TLD to own.

One new development is on the horizon. It seems that major companies will at some time soon be able to register "dot their corporate name", such as: .sears; .macys; .costco; .walmart etc. Whether that will extend to ".enzospizzeria" or ".moshesjewishdeli" remains to be seen!

GLOSSARY

Auto Responder: This is program (such as found at the popular aweber.com) that automatically detects the receipt of an email and replies to the sender with a prepared response letting them know their message has been received. These programs can be set up in a user's control panel.

Backups: Data from you that your Web hosts copy (typically once a day) in case of a loss of data situation. Backups allow hosts to easily restore lost data. Be certain your host offers backup.

Bandwidth: The amount of information transferred both to and from a website or server during a prescribed period of time. This is usually measured in "bytes". Hosting companies generally offer packages that come with different bandwidth transfer limits per month.

Blog Hosting: These are special scripts that let users automatically post new information to a website.

Browser (or "Web Browser"): A computer program used to view and interact with the content of Web pages on the internet.

Co-Location: When a user owns his/her own Web server, but houses it in the hosting provider's facilities for easy management, a high-speed connection, security, backup power and technical support, said user is "co-locating".

Control Panel: A Web-based application that allows you to manage various aspects of your hosting account. This includes uploading data and files, adding email accounts, changing contact information, installing shopping carts and/or databases and viewing statistics

Dedicated Hosting: When you rent or lease your own Web server that is housed at a hosting provider's facilities for easy management, a high-speed connection, security, backup power and technical support, you are buying dedicated hosting.

Disk Space: The amount of space available for you to house your website files on your host's server.

Domain Name: An address assigned to a website for identification purposes that can be translated by a domain name server into a server's IP address that includes a top-level domain.

Domain Name System: Keeps a database of domain names and their corresponding IP addresses, so that when a user searches for a domain name, the request can be routed to the server where the desired website resides

Domain Parking: The act of holding your domain name on a hosting server without the service provider requiring that you have a corresponding website up and running

Domain Registrar: A company responsible for managing your domain names and helping you secure the rights to a specific domain name you wish to purchase.

File Transfer Protocol (FTP): A commonly used method for exchanging files over the Internet by uploading or downloading files to a server. (An example would be "cuteFTP".)

Filename Extension: A tag that appears at the end of each file name. It consists of a dot and then three or four letters that signify the type of file and format.

Hypertext Markup Language (HTML): The cross-platform language in which the majority of Web pages today are written. Codes are interpreted by browsers to be properly formatted for visitors. It is relatively easy and helpful to learn, but not entirely necessary.

Hypertext Transfer Protocol (HTTP): This is the primary protocol for transferring and receiving data on the Web. It involves a browser connecting to a server, sending a request that specifies its capabilities and then receiving the appropriate data from the server in return. (In general you do not need to type this in to your browser before typing in the domain name.)

Internet Protocol (IP): Sets of rules and regulations agreed upon internationally for all internet functions.

Managed Hosting: A system whereby you own or lease a server that is located with a service provider. All of its management needs are taken care of by on-site personnel beyond your need to input or control anything.

Root Server: Servers containing software and data necessary for locating name servers containing authoritative data for top level domains.

Secure HTTP (SHTTP): An HTTP protocol that uses encryption to protect the traffic between the server and browser.

Servers: These are specially-networked computers that handle client requests including Web pages, data, email, file transfers and more

Shared Hosting: A system in which multiple clients and websites share a single server. Each account has specific limits on how much space they get and how much data they can transfer. This is the most basic and affordable type of hosting. The downside is if one client manages to crash the servers you go down too!

Shopping Cart: Software that lets website visitors select, add and remove products and pay for them online. This software can automatically calculate extra price considerations, such as tax and shipping. It then sends all of the information to the merchant once the transaction is complete.

Site Builder: An application offered by most hosting service providers. It allows you to create a website from scratch based on predesigned templates without requiring knowledge of HTML. The finished sites then run on the host's servers and can be accessed and used through any Web browser.

Static IP: A unique and unchanging IP address given to a website by the hosting provider.

Subdomains: These are third-level domains, addresses that replace the typical "www". This sends visitors to special URL (i.e. subdomain.website.com) that requests data from a different directory within the original website.

Support: Technical help provided by Web hosting companies, usually via phone or email, to correct any problems that customers may encounter.

Telnet: Standard internet protocol for accessing remote systems, such as Web servers

Top-Level Domain (TLD): The domain name element to the far right of the address (i.e. .com, .net or .org). See Addendum above.

Traffic: The data being transferred over a network, typically between the browser and server

Uniform Resource Locator (URL): This is your "domain name". It is the standard for giving the address of a resource on the World Wide Web that makes up your Web page's full unique address using alphanumeric characters.

Unmanaged Hosting: This is a system whereby you own or lease your own server and are fully responsible for the management of it. This includes troubleshooting, maintenance, applications and security, and is not recommended for anyone who is not an industry professional.

Uptime: The amount of time in a 24-hour period in which a system is active and able to service requests. Most hosts claim 99%+.

Web Hosting: This is the service that provides a physical location, space and storage, connectivity and services for websites that allow your files to be accessed and viewed by internet users. Sites are created and then uploaded to a Web hosting service provider's server. Some services provided include email addresses, free site builders and databases, among many other things.